The Poetry of
Yorifumi Yaguchi

The Poetry of Yorifumi Yaguchi

A Japanese Voice in English

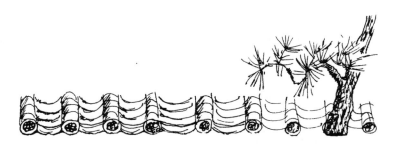

edited by Wilbur J. Birky

Good Books

Intercourse, PA 17534

800/762-7171 • www.GoodBks.com

Acknowledgments

"Grandpa" was first published in *London Magazine*.

"By the Memorial Gate," a collaborative poem by Yorifumi Yaguchi and William Stafford, was first published in *The Christian Science Monitor* on December 4, 1984. The poem appears in this collection by permission of The Estate of William Stafford.

"Listening to a Storyteller: In Memoriam William Stafford," a collaborative poem by Yorifumi Yaguchi and Robert Bly, was first published in *Poetry* magazine. The poem appears in this collection by permission of Robert Bly.

The line drawings on the title page and back cover are by Judy Wenig-Horswell.

The cover photograph is by Wilbur J. Birky.

Design by Dawn J. Ranck

ORDINARY DAYS
Copyright © 2006 by Good Books, Intercourse, PA 17534
International Standard Book Number-13: 978-1-56148-524-6
International Standard Book Number-10: 1-56148-524-1
Library of Congress Catalog Card Number: 2006006867

Library of Congress Cataloging-in-Publication Data

Yaguchi, Yorifumi, 1932-
[Poems. Selections]
The poetry of Yorifumi Yaguchi : a Japanese voice in English / edited by Wilbur J. Birky.
    p. cm.
"More than half of the poems originally written in Japanese..."--Email from publisher.
    ISBN-13: 978-1-56148-524-6 (pbk.)
    ISBN-10: 1-56148-524-1 (pbk.)
    I. Birky, Wilbur J. II. Title.
    PL865.A475A6 2006
  895.6'15--dc22   2006006867

Table of Contents

Introduction

The life and work of Yorifumi Yaguchi are unique and, in some respects, represent apparent contradictions. He is a personal witness to war who has become an active peacemaker. He is a compelling Japanese voice in the English language. He is both poet and preacher. He is a Buddhist become Christian and Mennonite. Since 1965, Yaguchi has had four overlapping careers: as professor of poetry and American literature at Hokusei Gakuen University, as pastor of several successive small Mennonite fellowships, as poetry editor for the Japanese poetry magazine in English *Poetry Nippon*, and as practicing poet. He continues in all of these roles to the present, including that of pastoral leadership in a small university fellowship.

A Brief Biographical Sketch

Yorifumi Yaguchi was born in 1932 and grew up in Ishinomaki and Yamoto, Japan—north of Tokyo and near the many tiny Matsushima islands, famed for inspiring the great Japanese haiku poets. Many of his "nature poems" reflect a strong fascination with the way nature inspires the smallest but most profound human feelings and insights. From his father he learned the Shinto way—including both emperor worship and the strong nationalism that drove much of Japan's military efforts during World War II. Yaguchi's poems show little attraction to this way, though a number of them deal directly with militarism's seductive and destructive power both in Japan and throughout the world.

But the Buddhism of Yaguchi's maternal grandfather is another matter. His grandfather's beautiful chanting of the Buddhist scriptures in the temple is a compelling part of Yaguchi's memory, and echoes of it are still heard in his poetry. His mother had a strong interest in Christianity and attended Christian worship, though she didn't formally profess a Christian faith. Yaguchi cites his mother's interest, together with his own study of T.S. Eliot at

3

Tohoko Gakuin University in Sendai, as instrumental in his later conversion to Christian faith and his baptism in 1958. He graduated with a B.A. from Tohoko Gaukuin in 1955, and then took up studies in English at International Christian University in Tokyo, where he did his M.A. thesis on Dylan Thomas and earned an M.A. in education in 1960.

From 1962-65 he studied at Goshen Biblical Seminary in Indiana, where he received his Bachelor of Divinity degree. While there, he wrote an account of his conversion to Christian faith, "The Bible Was Nonsense to Me" (published in J.C. Wenger, ed., *They Met God*, Scottdale, PA: Mennonite Publishing House, 1964). His poem "Someone," appearing in Section V (page 109) of this collection, is the most dramatic, if quite symbolic, representation of this conversion in his poetry: "a word like an ax" flung from the heavens to pierce "my unprepared heart."

During Yaguchi's three years in seminary, he not only studied Bible and theology but was also writing poetry. He published in Goshen's literary magazine *Foolscap*, as well as in national church publications such as *Christian Living* and *The Mennonite*. During this time he also wrote many of the poems found in his first book, *A Shadow* (1966). And in seminary he developed his enduring commitment to the way of peace.

The untimely death by cancer of his first wife, Reiko, in 1970 resulted in the poetic laments found in his second volume of poetry, *Resurrection* (1972). Two young sons to this marriage were lovingly raised by Yorifumi and his second wife, Mitsuko, whom he married in 1971, and whose contagious love makes her a valuable partner in Yaguchi's pastoral leadership in Sapporo.

After studies in the U.S., both sons are now professors of English in Japan. Yobu is Professor of English and Peace Studies at Shirayuri Women's College in Sendai and is the father of Yori's one grandson, Isaya, and one granddaughter, Ruka. Yujin is Professor of American Studies at Tokyo University. While Yorifumi Yaguchi is now officially retired from his professorship at Hokusei, he continues to teach poetry part-time at Hokkaido Bunkyo University in Sapporo.

Over the years Yaguchi developed close and significant relationships with many poets, especially American poet William Stafford, with whom he shared a love of nature and a concern for peace. The two corresponded, visited each other a number of times, stimulated each other's writing, and even collaborated in poetry writing (see page 119).

Yaguchi also shared a common spiritual calling and poetic vision with Welsh poet R.S. Thomas, whom he visited several times and with whom he corresponded for more than 25 years. Yaguchi has collaborated in the translating and publishing of a book of Thomas's poems in Japan.

In addition, appointed as a Fellow by the American Council of Learned Societies, Yaguchi spent a year (1976-77) at SUNY Buffalo, where he was a close associate of American poets Robert Creeley and Denise Levertov, and made significant contact with Robert Bly, Gary Snyder, Alan Ginsberg, and others (see page 118).

While I was a young boy growing up in Oregon during World War II, vaguely aware of blackouts to protect U.S. soil from potential Japanese bombing raids, Yaguchi was dodging U.S. strafing and bombs by hiding in coal mines and diving into rice paddies. Then came the day of the horrific blast in Hiroshima, and the news of national defeat that the young Yori heard at school in the crackling radio voice of his emperor. Far from destroying his poetic gifts, these wartime experiences give sharp focus to his poetry. (For the early personal story of the impact of World War II on Yaguchi, the reader is referred to his own essay, "What the War Did for Me," in the Spring 1986 isssue of *Festival Quarterly.*)

I first met Yaguchi-san in passing in the early 1960s when he was a student at Goshen Biblical Seminary in Indiana. My wife and I later hosted him in our home in 1976 when he was featured in the distinguished S.A.Yoder Memorial Lecture series at Goshen College. But our deeper encounters began in 1977 when he and his wife Mitsuko, together with sons Yobu and Yujin, became our next-door neighbors and gracious cultural and language lifeline during my sabbatical year at Hokusei University in Sapporo. There I learned firsthand of Yaguchi's deeply held commitment to poetry, to peace, and to the lifelong work of wrestling words to the page and the Word to a warring world.

Yaguchi has made an important contribution to studies in American literature in Japan through his additional translations. He has translated and published a book of Anne Sexton's poems in Japanese, as well as Cid Corman's *Selected Poems*, and joined with others in translating John Hollander's *Selected Poems*. He has published three books of his own essays on American writers for a Japanese audience: *Aspects of American Poetry, Words Making Sounds Together*, and *Landscape Through the Windows of English and American Poetry*.

Less literary of his translations into Japanese include the following books: Mark Hatfield, *Between a Rock and a Hard Place*; Jean Vanier, *Eruption to Hope*; and with his son Yobu, John Howard Yoder's *Body Politics*. In Sapporo he has hosted many American authors for readings and presentations. In addition, one of Yaguchi's Japanese books of poetry, *A Tree Staying Awake*, has been translated into Chinese and is awaiting publication by the Dalien University of Foreign Languages, which has already published some of his essays.

Some of Yaguchi's poetry has inspired several award-winning musical compositions by Canadian composer Jacques Desjardins, who has set the text of seven of his poems to music in two cycles; one is titled "The Yaguchi Cycle" and the other "Of Wind and Waves."

Individual poems have been published not only in Japan and the U.S., but also in England, Australia, Israel, Greece, India, and China. (Readers who are interested in further discussion of the poetry and influence of Yorifumi Yaguchi are referred to my own essay in the October 2003 issue of *Mennonite Quarterly Review*, "Yorifumi Yaguchi: International Poet and Prophet of Peace," a slightly longer version of the paper presented at the October 2002 conference on "Mennonite/s Writing: An International Conference" held at Goshen College, Goshen, Indiana.)

Yaguchi's Poetry Publications in English

Yaguchi is first a poet in the Japanese language. Fewer than half of his poems are in English, and he continues to publish in Japanese. A few of his poems in English Yaguchi originally wrote in English; most he translated himself. Other primary translators of his work have been Ross L. Bender for all of the 51 poems in *Jesus* (1989), and Mary Cender Miller with assistance from Sue and Wesley Richards for 16 of the poems in *Resurrection.* Miller has also translated a few of his other poems and essays.

As editor of this book I have selected nearly half of his more than 300 poems in English and have indicated in the text which poems were translated by Bender and Miller. Five primary books of his poetry exist in English, all currently out of print. Still in print are 30 poems selected by Good Books for publication in *Three Mennonite Poets* (1985).

Following are the primary sources and themes of the poems selected for this collection.

- *A Shadow*, 1966, 50 poems, published in Japan, gathers many of the poems written while Yaguchi was studying at Goshen Biblical Seminary from 1962-65. Most of these poems have long been out of print; only eight of them appear in later volumes. The first 18 poems are on war, a theme that continues throughout Yaguchi's career. This volume also contains some of his best poetry in English, including many "nature poems," as well as many of the poems depicting Yaguchi's childhood encounters with World War II and its aftermath in Japan. These poems are extensively represented in this book.

- *Resurrection*, 1972, 24 poems, is comprised of intensely personal laments written as his first wife Reiko suffered and died of cancer in 1970. In these poems' pain, they are similar to a number of the more existential poems that appear in the "Horizon" section of this collection, though they are much more obviously personal. Three of them were written by Reiko herself. I have included only two poems from *Resurrection*.

- *How to Eat Loaches*, 1984, 64 poems, is his longest volume. Like *Shadow*, it includes both "nature/enlightenment" and "war" poems. These portray the poet's wonder and his struggle with words, and they also include some of his most "raw" poems dealing with "beasts" and sexual themes. This volume's title, *How to Eat Loaches*, is also the title of the poem most frequently selected for publication among all of Yaguchi's poems. This poem appears in the "War and Peace" section of the present volume.

- *Jesus*, 1989, 51 poems, is somewhat atypical. Most of these poems were originally written as part of a series of meditations for the Protestant church in Japan, and then were translated by Ross L. Bender. A number of them depict imagined and often disturbing encounters of selected New Testament figures with Jesus: Mary, Peter, Lazarus, the "Demoniac," a Roman soldier, Judas, the two on the road to Emmaus. So while these are much more "biblical" than are most of Yaguchi's poems, many of them carry the recognizable elements of surprise, wonder, shock, and incarnation.

- *A Forlorn Dog*, 1993, 41 poems, is again more typical Yaguchi. It returns to some of his primary themes: nature, violence, and war in a variety of forms, and some of the haunting poems found in the "Horizon" section of this collection. It includes a number of poems published previously, especially from *How to Eat Loaches.*

- Other sources. For more recent poems, there are several significant additional sources, especially the *Journal of Hokkaido Bunkyo University.* In No. 1, 2000 are "11 English Poems," and in No. 5, 2004 are 19 poems published as "God of War and Other Poems." The latter are among his most recent and deal with a variety of war themes, including the haunting nightmares or war-derived dementia of now-aging Japanese participants in World War II—both men and women.

Yaguchi has also forwarded to me a number of additional poems, both published and unpublished. I have also included some uncollected poems that appeared in *Poetry Nippon*, the English poetry journal in Japan for which Yaguchi has served as poetry editor for nearly 40 years. And I have selected a few previously unpublished poems, mostly based on World War II experiences, found in the Archives of the Mennonite Church located at Goshen (IN) College.

Thematic and Chronological Organization

I have arranged the poems in this collection in six sections by theme, though of course any given poem may include multiple themes. Within each thematic section the poems are arranged approximately by the era of their writing—so that each section begins with early poems first written or published in the 1960s and ends with more recent poems from near or after 2000.

Silence, Section I, presents some of the more traditional "nature" poems. The narrator imagines himself as a tree, a bird, a whale, a mosquito, a praying mantis, or an old woman "walking with the autumn sky on her back." These poems present surprising encounters, a sudden illumination, or an unexpected point of "silence" in which the narrator touches the mysterious, the eternal. Sometimes these poems may be slightly comic, as in "I didn't know/ I was a tree/ till I tried to/ walk . . . " Sometimes they may connect directly to animist traditions of Hokkaido's native Ainu people as in "Mukkuri," or to the ritual silence of the traditional Japanese tea ceremony, or to a Buddhist "ah" that "disturbs/ my silence/ like the explosion/ of a/ temple bell."

Sometimes they are dreamlike or slightly askew, as with a bird that suddenly discovers it has no wings, or a tree that runs. There is even an aggressive silence as in the silent rows of marble Buddhas observed in a casual museum visit, Buddhas whose power the narrator thought he had left behind long ago, now unexpectedly beckoning him with their haunting and silent power.

Child of War, Section II, is somewhat autobiographical. It presents vignettes of childhood encounters with World War II in Japan: the tactile sights, sounds, smells, and sordid aftermath of war. Here Yaguchi flees toward mountain caves in the wake of B-29s appearing as "streams of black shades." Here he discovers a child on the road "Stretched out like a dead frog." Returning home at night with his parents, he finds an American soldier with an innocent face and muddy boots sleeping in a family bed. He watches as classmates "innocently" play prostitute. He writes of a grandpa's nocturnal nightmares of war many years later.

The point of view shifts rapidly from the small child to young women, to school teachers, to parents, to the shockingly innocent play of children, to uncles, to occupation soldiers.

Horizon, Section III, is likewise haunting, but is decidedly more existential—as if the poet is exploring a tangible absence, the deep silence in the wake of the noise of war. These poems seem to trace the line from a wounded experience to the distant horizon—sometimes vacant, sometimes almost touchable. Tracks left by a pair of ice skates stretch toward infinity. A surrealistic leaking closet, or ordinary fox tracks in the snow, intrude upon him from somewhere beyond. A lost kite, a silence, a faint breeze, footsteps beyond the door, distant waves of grass, a shadow, an echo, a voice—all haunt his memory, his fears, his hopes. The breath of a "forlorn dog" disturbs his consciousness and may point forward to the "presence" suggested by the following section.

Breath of God, Section IV, to some extent seems to answer the absence of the "Horizon" poems with "presence." Tea is poured mysteriously into his cup. Leaves quiver. And the more explicit Jesus poems graphically explore biblical stories and disturbing enigmas. A Roman soldier just doing his duty at the crucifixion wonders vaguely what the fuss is all about. A doomed Judas simply plays out his destined role in a cosmic drama he does not understand. The man who had "passed by on the other side" gets a glimpse into heaven, and is amazed to recognize the wounded man he had left lying by the side of the road.

The reluctant Jeremiah/Yaguchi finds himself possessed of prophetic voices that "fly out as arrows of fire."

Words Made Flesh, Section V, explores both the power and the elusiveness of words—in ordinary communication, in the calling of the poet, and in the essence of the Word.

There is the wonder of a child who first realizes that words passing out of his mouth can command action in others. There is the awed sense of words penetrating the sacred silences of the universe, or slicing like a razor, or sometimes turning into gravestones as if killed by the poet's efforts. The poet finds that words may provide bridges to the past or to "the world beneath sound." He senses the revolutionary power of the word/Word to "cut to pieces/ the night's empty sky."

This section ends with three collaborative poems, including one created together with his close poetic friend William Stafford and one written in collaboration with Robert Bly "in memoriam" upon the death of Stafford.

War and Peace, Section VI, frequently smarts with the sharp arrow of satire. War is a sport like deer-hunting, or is easily shut out by the willful deafness of the rich dancing at a party. Yaguchi's most frequently published poem, "How to Eat Loaches," is a sly exploration of how an innocent medicinal act turns into a major shock of recognition.

These poems range in subject from the tainted marble of colonial oppression in Westminster Abbey, to the atomic blast in Hiroshima, to "bony fingers" on the trigger in the Prague of 1968, and on to September 11 and the global war fervor in its wake. But this section also includes the unwitting cultural violence of well-meaning but ignorant missionaries and the apocalyptic nightmare of the dead rising up to bear arms.

This section on war and peace draws toward its close with three deeply contrasting poems. The first, in a sharply satiric mode, presents Lucifer as the maestro conducting a mighty chorus whose crescendo of war frenzy envelops the whole globe. In contrast, the next poem leaves us with the pathos of war's aftermath: a "maimed

11

orchestra of wingless grasshoppers" and "snails with broken shells" in the poet's own garden. Also implied is the fervent hope expressed in the final poem: that the word/Word will be allowed to do its work in the cause of peace on earth.

The reader is invited to find his or her own order, or connection, as the words on the page stir the memory, the heart, the deepest longings of the human spirit. Welcome to the world of Yaguchi-san: poet, teacher, editor, translator, pastor, husband, father, and friend who says that "I write today as if it were my last word. I write today as if I die tomorrow."

Wilbur Birky, editor
Goshen College
Goshen, Indiana

Section I:

Silence

*"My grandfather was a Buddhist priest.
I used to spend lots of time in his temple . . .
[he] often appears in my poetry."*

In the Mist

a drop fi-
nally falls

from the edge of
a leaf

. . . then
the faint

tremblings
of the leaves

silence*

in a far
place
I do not even know
a
leaf
falling down
like a silence
on the mirror
of the lake
making few
wavelets
hardly seen

ah
that sound
disturbs
my silence
like the explosion
of a
temple bell

This poem became the inspiration for an award-winning musical composition, "Cycle Yaguchi," by composer Jacques Desjardins. Other poems by Yaguchi set to music by Desjardins are "In the Mist" (page 14), "In the Wood" (page 22), "Into Waves" (page 23), "Words" (page 105), "Many Winds" (page 105), and "Gravestones" (page 106).

A

drop
from the moon . . .

and the end-
less

spreading a-
cross the pond . . .

faintly shaking the
waterlilies

one
after another

A

thin leaf
bends
heavily
and
lightly
and
lightly
and
heavily
as a dragonfly
tries to
perch
on it
and tries
to perch
on it

Each Time

the float
makes a slight move,

a dragonfly flies
up and up

and the sky and the mountains
almost crumble

A Fish

in the rock
a big fish,
still as a stone,
strains its ears,
trying hard to
learn how it's
going outside,

while outside
I
stand immobile,
holding my breath,
trying hard to
learn how it's
going inside.

A Tree

I didn't know
I was a tree
till I tried to
walk . . .

In a Wood

the red, full moon
is caught
in the spider's web

the web is fluttering,
the trees are rustling and
there is the strained

breath
of the spider watching hard
all excited.

A Bird

While flying
I doubted for a moment
that I was a bird.

I turned my head
only to find
I had no wings and

the next moment
I started to
fall . . .

A

withered leaf
hanging on a twig
heavy as the earth

A Skeleton Bird

A skeleton bird
Flying with its wings stretching out
Is frozen to the sky at night

Trout

Trout flying like
Arrows up the surging
Stream in the stone
Jump high up above rocks
Out of the stone
Hit violently
The water
Are shaking the night
Like a small boat.

Mukkuri

—a simple, small musical instrument of the Ainu people—

Water begins to flow
In the room, which soon
Comes to be a big stream, and
We are sitting in the water
Like rocks, around which fishes
Are swimming with fins rustling,
And from the upper stream
Down flowing is a canoe
With an old Ainu and a girl.

Tea Ceremony

Any action of making the tea,
Any action of tasting the tea is
The dance
Producing eternal stillness,

While through one or two
Leaves of words
Birds are flying from one heart
To the other most

Frequently in this small
Tea hut made of
Thin branches of trees and of bamboos,

In which lies something big as
The ocean, and the time born out of the
Stone is turning slowly around the silent two.

In the Wood

Leaves piling up at their feet
the trees stand naked. There is no
wind shaking the branches, no birds chirping.

Standing here, I hear a streamlet
creeping quietly like a snake,
a sound I never noticed during green times.

. . . there is a deep
old well
in a woman,
whose dark water
always reflects
ancient stars
among mossy rocks

. . . there is a big
black
fish in it,
vigorous yet
immobile like a rock,

watching . . .

. . . suddenly it
moves,
diving deeper
than her depth,
coming back and
jumping up
above the water . . .

. . . embracing her,
i feel its every
movement and
hear its heavy splashing
echoing
far down,
the water being
shaken

Into Waves . . .

While Shaving

I suddenly realize
I have no face,
what there is
is a dark hole
and the dark wind
is winding out,
blowing my hair,
and now,
hard as I may try,
I can't even remember
what kind of face
I used to have
if ever I had.

A Woman

naked
is lying
deep
in the grass
on a mountain
with the red
full
moon
between her
thighs

an egyptian mummy

in the eyes of an
egyptian mummy
is seen an
ancient
sky of
blue

in the height of which
an eagle is
flying
motionless

Praying Mantis

This morning I saw a male
praying mantis being
eaten by his female.

I could almost hear his
wild shout of ecstasy
as his wife ate him

and his joy seemed to increase
the more his body was
violently bitten along.

The complete trance of
self-oblivion came at the moment
when his last part was bitten.

—Tonight when I am exhausted
after our long and violent intercourse,

I think of the male mantis,
wondering if his swallowed body
was digested or is still praying in her.

In A Field

Smoke is going up—
A white thread hanging from the heavens.

Something

moved
just a little

in the grass
beside my foot.

"Rat or snake!" I thought,
drawing back.

But that was all—
And the world deepened.

Even Before I Was Born

There is a huge tree in me
with its roots spread
deep into the earth, pulsating.

Its boughs unfold their branches
all across the sky and breathe
among thick leaves.

There is a time when someone
shakes the tree in big waves,
then the wind rises up in folds,

the cloud is torn and blown,
birds start crying and I cling
to the trunk with all my might.

The tree keeps living in me
even after I die . . . .The small trembling
of its leaves keeps moving me.

A Mosquito

A mosquito
perched on my arm
and put its
needle into my flesh
and began to suck
the red juice.

Its face
gradually
turned shiny,
saying, "Ah
how nice
to live . . . "

I became so
itchy but tried
hard to endure,
while it became so intoxicated
it almost started singing . . .

A Black Cat

A black cat was lying
on the fence of the entrance to a park.
A crowd of ravens found it and
quickly flew near. They perched
on the branches just above the cat
and stared it down.

One came down almost
to its back and flew up.
Then the others followed and flew down and up
one by one. But the cat never moved.
Only its gold eyes were ardently burning,
while the ravens were making hoarse sounds.

Some tried to almost stab it
but the cat was still a sculpture.
After a long noisy while, they finally flew
away. The willow branches began to wave
and cicadas sang loudly. Then
the cat sluggishly stood up and slowly walked away.

A Tree

There is a tree
which alone holds
the falling sky.
Its arms bend and
almost break.
Its veins are about to
jump out from its legs.

Somewhere in it
cicadas are hiding
and lightly sounding
their notes.

Buddhas

In the Asian rooms
of the New York Metropolitan Museum,
Buddhas dwell, seeing us
with eyes half-way closed.

Some are huge, while
some others are so tiny
that you can even hold them in your hands.
Some stand still, while
others sit still. None of them
have a bent back. All of them
are meditating, with the tops
of their heads pointing heavenward.

One day I walked into their forest.
Then my grandfather, a Zen monk, who had been
living in me, tried to stop and chant a sutra
in front of each one, as he had done while he was alive.

Since I was a converted Christian, commanded
not to worship idols,
I tried hard to persuade him
to move more quickly,
but he was reluctant.
I tried to force him to become a tourist or
an art lover who looked at them only
as pieces of art and casually walked away.

—At last we finished our round
but he still wanted to linger. So I took his hand
and pulled him hard
out through the exit.

Then behind us
all Buddhas began to utter
their silent voices together
just like cicadas in the midsummer.

A Tree Staying Awake

The wood behind us is fast asleep
and the pillars of gigantic silence spread.
Not even one leaf trembles . . .
But in the most interior of the wood

is a tree always staying awake;
it shakes its body as if it were about
to start to run, its eyes burning, its mane
waving, it's forelegs lifting, neighing . . .

The ripened orange of the moon now
climbs to the top of the heavenly stairs,
while in the bottom of the earth
crouches the time, never moving.

It is this very moment when the tree will
cut off its invisible rein to run.
I listen with my eyes wide open,
expecting it to start at any moment and

run like a gust of wind with its hooves
sounding high. Then all the other trees
will start running in response and
the whole world will shake and stir.

The dead, small ones

Fallen leaves are blown
in time's shore, where
the dead bodies of insects are drowned . . .

Dragonflies without tails, cicadas
with their intestines all gone, grasshoppers
with only their heads remaining, the shells of snails . . .

I disturb the leaves and
gather the fragments of the dead; then
my palms gradually become their mound.

A Scapegoat

In a corner of the darkening wilderness
A goat was standing alone despondently.
Its hair was plucked out and numerous
Purple scars spread across his body.

Frightened first with my appearance,
He did not show any sign of moving away.
It must have been a goat recently
Driven out of a nearby village.

The goat who bore
All the guilt of the village people
And had been punished by their god for them,
Thus soothing him and redeeming them.

It was surely a most handsome
and healthy goat
Who had never known any female,
But now it had become impure and dirty.

The moment our eyes met,
It tried to approach me. "Don't come!
Go away! My traveling
Has no end!" I repeated,

But he wouldn't go away. I hurried;
He trotted after me.
I threw him an angry gaze;
Then he turned his eyes away but never left.

I have begun to wonder if the village people
And their god have both become happy
Because of this goat, who
Now is so near me that we can touch each other.

What Shirasawa Nabe, an Ainu woman who died at the age of 84 in 1993, told me shortly before her death

How many songs do I know?
I cannot tell . . . The people often came to me
from the ministry of education and
recorded my singings

but not all. My closet is full
of their recorded tapes,
which are probably only 60 percent.
They asked me to remember and sing all of them,

but I could not. To be honest,
I myself do not know
how many Yukaras are in me.
I had learned them listening when a child.

I do not know how old they are.
But when the morning sun comes into my room,
a song comes out of my mouth
most naturally like birds' singings.

Different songs fly out of me
according to my mood in different situations;
songs I never thought of knowing . . .
songs I could never remember when asked . . .

A Whale

Someone sometimes asks, "What would you like to be
if you are to be born again?" And some happy people answer,
"Of course, a human being! And I want to repeat
what I have done." But I myself want to be
a whale if I have to be born again.

I want to become that gigantic body that swims
the northern sea like its own playpen.
I want to go down 1,000 meters in an instant,
then go up straight to the surface, to jump up into the sky,
to fall, to splash the water all over.

Sometimes a whaleboat with ant-like people on it
will appear. I will keep a safe distance from it
and seduce it to the cliff by the sea.
When the boat is shaken like a chip of wood in the storm,
I will swim under the raging waves unaffected.

When the time of death draws near, I will lie
in the whales' grave at the dark bottom. I will peacefully
close my eyes and remember those bright days I lived,
faintly feeling the waves moving far above.
The thick quietness will enwrap me.

The deep sea fish will come lightly to me and peck softly
at my flesh. I will become a part of their lives.
The remaining flesh
will become a part of the sea. Only the skeleton will remain.
The deep sea fish will swim through it. But that skeleton, too,
will decompose in time and then all myself
will become the sea itself.

Nine One-Line Poems

In the grass the fallen trees turn around.

Each time the fallen tree breathes, the grass moves faintly.

The big winds chase around to catch a fallen leaf.

A wrecked ship floats on the waves of the cosmos.

Ah, a butterfly! Flying around the waterfalls.

As I climb up, a mountain walks down the trail.

The winds blush in full bloom all over the mountain.

In the field a child urinates against the setting sun.

An old woman walks with the autumn sky on her back.

Section II:

Child of War

"The first air raid came in the middle of the night . . .
We were a long, silent line.
Overhead hundreds of B29s . . .
Sirens wailed . . .
we arrived at the mountain and entered a gaping hole,
the mouth of an abandoned mine."

I Still Remember . . .

I still remember that night when I was awakened
At midnight and could not go to sleep again.
It roared like a thunder through the whole night
And my house was shaken and I was trembling in between
Wetting my pillow with tears.

Early next morning adults were out in the street
Talking to each other in low voices, saying
That there were so many, so many tanks
Passing through the street last night . . . .

Our Breakfast Table

Our breakfast table was unusually quiet. Father told us that the
war had begun. Parents didn't talk much, and we didn't ask
much. For a grace, Father prayed that our country might win the
war by the mercy of Japanese gods and the Japanese emperor.

In the school we were standing in rows in the playground, and
then, a low voice came out of an old radio which was set in
front of us. His accent was so unnatural. It was announced that
he was our emperor, our living god. It was the first public decla-
ration of war against the USA and Britain.

First Air Raid

My hand is bound up with
Mother's, which is like a steel wire
Pulling me most violently
In spite of my will.

Before us and after were
Gigantic streams of black shades
Moving silently toward the mountain,
Which stands darker than the night.

We see our friends
But we never salute,
Our neighbors see us
But they never smile.

We hurry up,
Leaving our acquaintances far behind
In order to get a safer shelter,
Then they pass us, far ahead.

Behind us the siren is
Unceasingly making gruesome sounds
And just above our heads swarms of
B-29s are flying with thunderous sounds.

The Coal Mine
—An Air Raid Shelter—

Darkness dwells in the coal mine all the time.
Small groups scatter here and there, and
People are warming themselves around
A few feeble gaslights.

Chill drops of water drip
Drip
Drip down
Like snakes from rocks
Round and above,
Wetting blankets and dresses.

They never move, they never talk,
But are squatting down like turtles,
Eating food as big as a fist.

A Boy

A boy is lying on the road,
Stretched out like a dried frog,
Spitting blood which is parched
And glued to the soil.

He who was running with joy,
Leaping with the first freedom he got
And laughing with the blue sky,
Is now lying silently and motionless
On this road, which is burning—afire
With the sun.

I Heard

I heard that in the Philippines Japanese soldiers
Ran over corpses of enemies with heavy trucks.

I heard that in Indonesia Japanese soldiers
Pierced wire into hands of enemies and soaked them in the sea.

I heard that in China Japanese soldiers
Pierced a pregnant woman with swords into her belly.

And whenever we heard these news
We leaped with joy.

It was in Autumn

It was in Autumn, when
The rice was as gold as the sunshine,
And I was walking
Alone in the field,
Toward my town,
Toward my house,
Leaving the black, chilly, wet,
Hiding cave far
Behind me and
I was singing,
I was leaping,
I was running,
I was laughing,
I was breathing
Deep
The clean, autumnal air,
Cool and nice. The rice
Smelled, smiled, locusts
Leaped, dragonflies
Flew round me and
Up in the blue,
Blue sky.

When suddenly,
A small black swarm
Of airplanes
Appears
Above the mountain, and
They come rapidly
To my town, and
One finds me,
Begins to chase
Me, and
I run,

Run
And run
Breathless
Into the rice field,
Hide myself
Deep among the rice
Lying in the water,
And it shoots me,
The machine-gun,
And shots with
Thunderous sound
Approach and
Pass just beside me
Ten inches away
From my right arm,
Splashing the water,
Whole upon my body.

I was lying
Trembling,
Forgetting myself,
I do not know how long,
But I felt it's a long,
Long time, and finally
It's gone, all planes were
Gone away, and I stood
Up, standing up
Continuously,
Looking toward the sky
Into which they disappeared.

One Day I Was Walking

One day I was walking
In the street, which was dead
As a stone. There was nobody,
Not even a dog there, and I
Was walking barefooted, and
The hot sun was beating down
On my hatless head.

The enemy planes passed
Our street like a summer shower just now.
There was a smell of gun powder,
But there was no sound, not even
A sound of birds, when
I heard, all of a sudden,
Music, quiet melody of Koto,
The classical Japanese instrument.

A sad, pathetic,
Yet unusually beautiful sound
Was coming
From an old hut
From an old radio,
Which I thought the owner forgot
To switch off when he ran away.

I forgot the danger and
Was standing in front of the hut,
Listening to this beautiful and
Calm music
Which was far from this world.

I was listening, forgetting the time,
And it seemed to be endlessly continuous, and
I was completely absorbed into it, when
A small, white cat
Approached me and rubbed its head
Around my feet and
Twined itself around my legs.

Father

Sudden, rain-like gunshots
Sowed the ground around us just now,
Splashing the sand. And
Father falls down
On the ground,
Father who had been standing before us
Like a huge rock
Falls down
So easily like a rotten tree.

Blood begins to gush out of him
Like a fountain,
Dyeing the soil around him.

He is dying,
Father is dying, who
Believed in the holy war, who
Believed Japan would surely win.
He who seemed to be as strong as
An iron bar falls down and now
Lies motionless before our eyes
And is fainting like a small girl.

We Now Know

We now know that
A Christian pastor
Interceded for blessings
On those soldiers
Who were about to fly
To the blue, blue sky of Hiroshima,

So that God of Christ
Might be with them
In this historical moment,
In that historical event,
So that God might assume
The salvation of the souls
Of those brave soldiers.

Now we feel we hear the pastor
Reading the Bible aloud,
Praying for them, and
We feel we hear the sound
Of the hearts of the soldiers
Beating violently high.

We Came Home Late

We came home late at night
And found our house lit,
And we saw in it
Big footsteps of mud
On *Tatami*, the Japanese floor mat.

And there we found an American soldier
Sleeping with a snore
In our bed
With uniform on
With muddy shoes on.

He was sleeping sound and deep,
With his breath smelling of wine,
And we looked into his face,
Which looked as innocent as
That of a schoolboy.

I Saw A Soldier

I saw a soldier as old as my father
Stealthily picking up like a chicken
One grain of rice after another, which
Were fallen and scattered in a stream,
And his uniform was as withered as
A dried cabbage.

And I saw an officer as young as my brother
With a long sword chiming,
With long, shiny, black boots squeaking,
In new military dress with medals glittering,
With a fat, apple-like face shining,
With big, mountain-like shoulders perking up,
With a chicken-breast,
Striding to and fro
Like a proud tiger
Among small cats.

A Shadow
—Or Hiroshima—

Look
At this stone-step,
Look at this
Shadow, man-shaped,
Printed on this stone.

Someone was resting here
In the shape of the "Thinking man" of Rodin,
And perhaps he was
Thinking,
Thinking deep something else,
Tired out by war, and was
Resting at 8:15 a.m.
On August 6, 1945.

Now here
Only his shadow is
Left
Exactly in his shape.
It is left
Here
As the image
Left in our heart
Which will never,
Never die out.

It Was in August

It was in August and we were made to stand
In rows on the school ground, and the hot sun
Was burning as sulfur above our heads. There was
No breeze, but a dull silence hung
All around us. Then we began to hear someone
Speaking through the radio set before us
With a dull, withered voice
With a sluggish intonation, which reminded me
Of a voice we had heard four years before.

He was weeping,
That man was weeping while speaking,
We did not know why, and we did not care
What he was speaking about, but we were
Struggling hard against
The burning heat and the terrible hunger,
And our fellow students fell on the ground
Thick and fast,
Before me
Behind me
And around me,
Losing consciousness,
And they were left there as they fell down
On the burning ground
While that man was talking,
Because that man was talking,
And his slumberous talk
Continued without end.

At length, his speech ended,
And all teachers were weeping
With tears filling their eyes,
Which we had never seen before.
We did not know what happened,
But we were only glad that
We did not have to be continuously
Standing under the hell-fire,
And then
One young teacher approached us and said,
"You do not understand, you
Do not understand what happened, do you?"
And went away with his head drooping.
But someone began to say here and there
That the war was over, that Japan lost it,
And this rumor spread like a fire
Among students, who were wondering
Why the gods did not intervene for Japan.

I Remember

I remember that
The first street-girl I saw
Was the sister of my good friend.
She had come to our house several times
During the war, when we suffered from the shortage
Of food, bringing in some vegetables and rice,
And she was fourteen or fifteen when I saw her
    in the street,
And she was a short, baby-faced girl.

I remember that
My friend was weeping
When we saw his sister
Walking along with an armed soldier
Hand in hand in the street.
His eyes were swollen with tears,
His hands were trembling
And his face turned white as paper.

I do not know where she is
And what she is doing now,
Living or dead, happy or unhappy,
But my friend
Killed himself,
Throwing himself down a steep cliff
Soon after we saw that scene.

Children Are Playing

Children are playing,
Playing prostitutes.

"I am the soldier,"
"I am the prostitute, then."

"Honey, I come to you every night."
"Then, I am your *only*."

Little children are playing
In the garden under the tree,

Hands in hands, lips on lips,
Pretending to go under a blanket,

And near them, parents are absorbed
In talking with prostitutes.

We, Her Pupils

We, her pupils, were looking,
Trembling with fear, at those
Soldiers violating our young
Lady teacher.

She was fighting, fighting
Like a butterfly, and we,
Her pupils, were only looking, doing
Nothing, being unable to move

Because of extreme fear,
Our teacher was shrieking, but
Soon fell down like a fallen petal
Among armed solders,

Under armed soldiers in a
Bamboo bush behind a
Shinto shrine and we,
Her pupils, were only looking,

Trembling almost to death, at
The terrible scene,
Doing nothing, not even
Trying to shout.

A Lonely Season

The day is dying down,
And the children are going home;
Then the world quiets down as in the wood.

That is all . . . .
But why does my heart ache so much?

Look at the face of this child
Left alone by the roadside,
Standing vacantly in the darkness
Which is rapidly growing up to surround him
Like a wall.
Look at its face.
It has no crossness anymore
Which it had while playing with the children.
But loneliness is
Flowing out of the face.

The night is falling upon him,
But the child is not going home.
Everybody is going home
Hurriedly
Even with tears on their cheeks,
But this child is not going home.

The child is gazing,
Leaning against the pillar,
Doing nothing,
But only gazing
In the mirror
At the face of its mother,
Which is gradually changing into
A face of some other woman.

After its mother is gone out,
The child is looking
Through the window at
The darkness, in which
Nothing is seen.
It is looking,
Never moving from the windowside,
Not talking back,
Nor smiling back,
But only gazing
At the darkness of
The outside world.

A Muzzle

"You follow me, will you?"
There was an irresistible power in his low voice.
He was a petty officer of the navy
With glasses on his dark face.
I was a freshman in a junior high school.

He took me to the backyard of the station
And accused me, saying "Didn't you realize
How many Japanese were killed
By American soldiers! How insolent you are
To talk to such a soldier in English!"

Then he slowly took out his black
Shining pistol and pointed its muzzle
At my face, which froze in that instant.
I tried hard to soften it in vain.
His finger on the trigger was about to cramp.

I closed my eyes with my heart pounding.
I didn't know how long, but
I couldn't bear it any longer.
I opened them a little and found
He was reluctantly lowering the muzzle.

Instead, his eyes were gazing at me;
Two deep dark holes. Even after some fifty years,
When I am talking with an American
In English, these two holes often
Take me back to that chill moment of despair.

That Child

That child is never attached to me,
How long the time may pass and
Whatever I may do, never
Will it be attached to me, and
I know in it the flame of malice
Is burning up like freezing ice.

With friendship I try to approach it,
Then it boils hostility like oil and
Draws back step by step, and should I
Approach more, it begins to peel its
Big, red eyes in its soiled face and
Attacks me full of hatred with a stick
In one hand and mud in the other.

That child is never attached to me,
How long the time may pass and
Whatever I may do, never
Will it be attached to me, and
I know in it the steel of
Bad temper is blowing like a whirlwind.

So finally I give it up and leave it alone.
Then the more its crossness grows, and it
Lets passing children cry, hits them with
Blue veins in its forehead, and to approaching
Adults it throws pebbles with a nonsense cry, and
At length, with tears full in its face, it
Dashes toward me with stones in its hands.

That child is never attached to me,
How long the time may pass and
Whatever I may do, never
Will it be attached to me, and
I know in it loneliness
Lies in the form of a desert.

At night I try to take a peep
Into its room through the closed door,
And it is crying, clenching its teeth
Hard, trying not to utter a crying voice,
And its leaf-like hands are
Hardened into iron and are tearing off
Without its notice the sheet on its bed.

But should I try to go in the room
To console it, it all at once
Stops to cry and raids me most
Furiously with its nails and brutal cry.

That child is never attached to me,
How long the time may pass and
Whatever I may do, never
Will it be attached to me, and
I know in it solitude
Is glittering with hungered eyes.

am I?

am I a cicada
pinned down only
dreaming of those intense
cries and flies in the summer days

not moving my wings lest
i should know I can't fly
but squatting down silently
waiting

in a dark chemistry room
for the footfall of someone
approaching
from beyond the corridor?

I

1. In Wonder

I am gazing
through the sight
at the deer

gazing all
at ease as if he knew
nothing about me,

sometimes looking en-
chantedly at him-
self in the water . . .
as my finger, closing, is

cramped a-
round the trigger . . .

2. In the Open

I am grazing
beside the lake
in the wood . . .

The grass is
soft
and sweet . . .

As the breeze
combs the water,
my body dissolves in the broken light . . .

And all
the while I am
feeling

The dark glaring eye
of the muzzle
set fast upon my back . . . .

A Deer

The bullets explode
and the powder smoke envelops
the trees in a far wood
in my sleep

And I am half dreaming of my sweetheart
and half hearing those faint sounds of
shooting and the confused footsteps of those
fleeing in all directions

And when all those sounds fade away
into the mud of my drowsiness,
suddenly!
breaking the curtain of resumed calmness

One wounded deer desperate
comes rushing toward me
with its eyes bloodshot
out of breath finally

Jumping violently into me
shattering
my peace and ease of drowsiness
irredeemably

Rats

One day a few blood-stained rats
Jumped suddenly out of my mouth and
Quickly ran away, as I gasped to watch them.

I looked into my stomach in a hurry,
And there! My intestines were all
Gone! But innumerable rats were running

Around, eating up everything.
"I've got to get rid of them before it's too late!"
I said to myself, almost fainting with horror.

But then, they began to jump out of my mouth,
One after another, and when I shut my jaws,
I bit into a swollen one, which dangles from my teeth.

At Midnight

I am awakened by
something es-
caping
from me

and I listen to
it
falling
far in-
to the dark

A Rescued Vietnamese Boy

For days we did not eat or drink.
Babies sucked withered breasts,
feebly crying, while my brother suddenly
burst into laughter and jumped into the sea . . .

Then one dawn we found a big fishing boat,
a Japanese one, near us, and we waved
and shouted, "*Tasukete!*,"* the word
Japanese salesmen taught us before the liberation . . .

But the boat, pretending not to notice us,
quickly went away and we were again floating
without any country to return to or to go to
and my family died one after another . . .

*"*Save us!*"

Meditating the Zen Way

Deep in the mountains
high on a rock I meditate Zen fashion
concentrating on the gentle movement of
leaves in the trees and gradually
sinking into oblivion, when

Brr, brr, brr, brrrr, brrr, a formation of
helicopters flies over, shaking the trees.
Controlling myself—the copters will pass on
like a rain shower—I again take up my Zen
posture—but, brr, brr, brr, brrrr, brrr, again—

"Clear your mind of mundane thoughts and
fire will be cool to the touch"—unlike the
monk's famous koan, nor able to attain to
the Zen wisdom "Sound is also silence,"
I jump to my feet and

Shake my fist at the copters
"Get outa here, dammit!
How can ya do Zen with all that!"
Maybe they can't hear me, but
They can read my gestures—

Without the slightest notice of me
brr, brr, brrr, brrrr
they come on, until passing overhead
some soldiers look down and
wave back

(translated by Mary Cender Miller)

Usually

I love peace
but when I wear a soldier's uniform
I begin to wish a war would happen
and to feel like killing
as many enemies as possible
by raiding them, if so ordered,
and dying willingly
for the sake of the Emperor
and our country.

Grandpa

Grandpa suddenly gets up at midnight and
shouts, "It's time!" and
throws off our *futon* and makes us get up and
sit in the living room.

After calling our names, he sits
before his desk with the blackboard behind and
begins giving a lecture he had repeated
for thirty years at a university.

We have to take notes on whatever he tells us
because during his lecture
he checks our notes carefully and
scolds us if they are not satisfactory.

His clouded eyes glitter,
his bent back straightens and
his mustache trembles like a float.
But the lecture finishes too soon.

He collapses and starts snoring, pissing
in his pants, his snot forming a bubble
on the end of his nose, and repeating in his sleep,
"The Kamikaze are coming!"

Who?

Who became a soldier?
My gentle uncle,
Who often took me fishing
And taught me how to hunt for mushrooms.

Who became a soldier?
Our neighbor Ichiro,
Who worked hard in the rice field
From early morning till night.

Who became a soldier?
Mr. Ryosuke, a keeper of cattle,
Who took his cows to the grassy field
Even on rainy days, gently whipping their hips.

In the front did they make a queue with others
In front of the huts, waiting
For their turn to spend a short time with
those conscripted Korean girls?

50 some years since the defeat of the war,
The long neglected victims, now aged women,
Finally showed up on TV, tremblingly
Exposed their shameful days of forced "comforting,"
while in our village one of the ex-soldiers
Is dedicated in Yasukuni Shrine as a war god,
The next one lost his memory and is senile, and the third one
Is enjoying his peace surrounded by his grandchildren.

A Military Song

When I am alone in a quiet place
I find myself humming
to myself a military song
learned when I was a child.

I think I am the
absolute pacifist
but in spite of my intention,
the song springs up

naturally out of my depth . . .
whenever I am unguarded or absentminded.

Section III:

Beyond the Horizon

*"Suddenly silence flies up in the form
Of a bird from a bush nearby."*

A Shadow

A shadow
Of someone
Standing
On the other side
Of the horizon
Is now
Almost
Touching my feet.

My Horse

Sometimes suddenly my horse gets up,
Jumping higher than my shoulders,
And begins to run violently shaking its mane

To the horizon, no,
Pointing to something invisible
Which lies far beyond the horizon,

Running like a whirlwind with its
Eyes brightly shining

Until at last it exhausts itself and lies down
Again upon grasses like crumbled sands.

A Skater

Somebody crossed
The ice-field in me
By the sharpest edge
Just now!

Surprised,
I turned my head
Into it quickly
But it's too late,

And only two lines
Were left continuous
Beyond the horizon on
The ice on which nobody
Had ever passed.

I Opened . . .

I opened the door of a house
Nobody lived in,
Then suddenly!
Lonely children ran out of it
And clung to me.

A Train

I hear a last train passing by
Far away through a desert field,
And now, my first train
Starts in my heart.

Moko-Chan
—A Sick Boy—

Moko-chan is standing alone
In the evening, looking at a
Train passing away. Putting
His hands in the pockets of his
Knee breeches, he won't move
From his place at all. And on his
Pale face hang two snivels
Like two blue pencils, and he
Is gazing at the distant night
Which is swallowing up the train.

When it becomes too late,
His brother comes to see him;
"Moko-chan, it's supper time
Already, it's too late now,
Let's go home . . . ," but Moko-chan
Won't listen to him, but is
Listening hard to a voice
Coming to him from the dark above.

Moko-chan,
What is it that is seen in your eyes?
What is it that is coming to your ears?
Little Moko is now pointing his finger up
To something in the darkened sky, while
His brother is trying hard to pull him by hand,
Persuading him with subdued voice, lest
They should be heard by passers-by.

A Stone

In a womb
A woman has a stone
Bigger than a loin, and
It makes her bone freeze.
She tries to warm it, but
It never warms, and this
Ancient stone grows colder and bigger
As she grows older.

Look at a girl
Who stopped running and
Never laughs any more.
And look
At an old woman
Sitting in a field
Looking at a horizon
With her heavy stone
Sinking deeper
Into the ground.

On Sunny Days . . .

On sunny days, when
I look down from this cliff
At the sea in a glance,
Not even a single shade of
A boat is seen, but
Now, when
This thick, milk-like fog
Stands like a curtain
All around, clearly
Appear in it numerous
Fishing boats full of flags
Of various colors of extravagancy
Approaching toward the harbor one after another.

Because . . .

Because my door was pleasantly knocked on,
I opened it to welcome my guest,
Expecting his cheerful smile.
But what rushed into me was
A black chill of frozen wind,
Laying waste my secret room.
It took me a thousand years
To warm it and bring it to order so that
I was born right again.

A Shadow

I know before I was born,
Even before I was conceived as a seed,
A shadow, stealing as a wind
Through a crack not existing
In the room in which
No secret of the night shines,
Came secretly into me
Without my even slightest knowledge:
The shadow which is far darker
Than my blood and is far larger
Than my body.
The moment it entered in me,
The sudden shriek of an appalling woman
Sounded in the street of the night,
And with it—the sound of a womb
Being wildly torn down ran
Like a flame, which woke me up
From the dream of the dead before I was born,
Even before I was conceived as a wind.

A Lonely Boat

After I go to sleep,
A boat leaves
From the harbor in my heart,
Full of lonely people,
Without any destination.

And on the beach are people
Who could not ride in it, and
They are seeing the boat of their beloved
Off disappearing
Into the horizon, with their bodies
Hardening from ripping cold and loneliness.

But next morning when I wake up,
I always find the boat wrecked out
On the sand, with numerous
Dead bodies, swollen with water,
And cries of lamentation fill the village,
Which wake me up in the morning.

But at night after I go to sleep,
The boat leaves again as usual
Full of lonely people
From the beach of my lonely heart,
Without any destination.

Then . . .

Then, the wave squatting down like a cat
Suddenly stood up, attacking me
With growling fangs, and at the same time
Voices were flying toward me from the bottom
Of the bottomless darkness, abundant voices
Echoing like a flood in a tunnel, and
I tried to catch their meanings, but
I couldn't understand them at all.

I closed my eyes and gazed at
The world of darkness and then
Gradually I saw that the sea and
The cliff were living together at the
Same height like twins in the belly,
And fishes were swimming from the water
Into the air freely, and birds were
Flying from the air into the water freely.

I closed my eyes firmer and gazed more
At the darkness and then I saw
That the world beyond the sea and the cliff
Was split like a womb and breathing most lively
Like a hatched egg with breathing red and
Blue veins, and from there the wind
Blowing in the stone is flowing toward me.

I hurriedly wave my arms which I had not
Into the sky which did not exist, and then,
In response to it, the chorus of fish
In the wave began to be heard, with which
The voiceless voice echoed like a shade
High above the sky all around.

Vacancy

Let this vacancy
sink
deep down
in me

and

let it stay
there
an old pond
forever.

The Kite

Children are looking up
Drawing in the string
After a kite
Which was suddenly swallowed up
Into the windless sky,
In spite of their will.

They draw and draw the string,
But the kite never returns,
And at last, they are tired of it,
Go home with sullen hearts,
Leaving a reeled string behind.

But after that
Somebody is in the darkness,
Drawing in the string
Quietly and continuously
After their lost kite,

And its sound is heard
Spreading around the world
Like a wind.

Tonight

From afar
a big foot
comes quietly

The grass ceases its rustling
Among the startled creatures
a silence

spreads
I close my eyes
and wait

(translated by Ross L. Bender)

A Surprise

When I breathed in deep,
everything around me
rushed into my mouth;

dancing butterflies, singing
cicadas, buzzing
bees, fragrant flowers . . .

When I breathed out deep,
all of them went out
and returned to their old places.

A Bird

Surrounded by the horizon,
I was standing in the middle of a field;
then a bird glided down
and perched on my outstretched finger.

I was pretending to be a tree;
it rested there a while and then
quickly flew up and away
leaving a small drop on the tip of my finger.

The Scrapped Vessel

I go into the belly
of a ship
whose intestines have been gouged out

and find its beams fallen,
its boards torn off,
clusters of shepherd's purse growing.

I close my eyes and hear
a faint breeze
moving through

bringing the sound
of the waves of grasses
from the other world.

Suddenly scraps of
old voices break off
and begin to fly around like butterflies.

A Narrow Road

I was taking a narrow road.
It didn't join a highway,
It bent and twisted
as it pleased.
It crossed a wooden bridge,
crawled beside a cliff,
wandered among trees,
climbed a descending mountain
and finally came to a look-out.

Underneath stretched
a sea of grass.
After a moment it
abruptly slipped
down the steep slope,
jumped into the waves
and disappeared.
In the offing
tall grasses were swaying
their slow crests of waves.

A Back Street

There is a back street only those
born there know of and I walk there
and see shabby houses squat
like decayed teeth along its narrow, bent road.

A jobless man is sunbathing,
looking up at the sky and grinning;
a prostitute without the paint on her face
is absentmindedly standing in a vacant lot.

An old man is tottering
like a baby just learned to walk;
a pickpocket who has just finished his job
helps wash clothes with the eyes of a sheep.

Whomever I meet I exchange
wordless greetings with and walk lazily along
and come to the grassy field,
on the other edge of which hangs the big sky.

The Closet

It was leaking from the closet.
I opened it just a little to see,
but water spurted out through the crack.
In a flurry I closed it, then many wet hands
tried hard to open it from inside and
I have been leaning like a rock to keep it closed.

My hair mixed with ashes, my eyes dim,
my hands numb—finally one day
I noticed it became quiet inside.
I summoned up my courage to open the door
and found there the dark peaks soaring
with stars spreading endlessly beyond them.

At That Time

Someone was approaching from beyond . . .
And his footsteps stopped
just in front of my door.

And I, holding my breath,
prepared for his
entering . . .

In this way a few
decades have passed, and yet
I'm still waiting

Because someone is still
standing there,
ready to come
in at any time.

Trash

Because people stepped on it,
I first thought it was a piece of trash.
Since it was not blown away,
I tried to pick it up, then

I found it had a thread-like root.
I tried to pull it out, but
it went deeper into the ground
with a small smoke of dust.
It became bigger as it
dived deeper and I now
tried harder to pull it out
with both of my hands.

Then some huge sound jumped
out of the ground and the place
around began to quake
and a big cliff appeared.

A dark world hung in it,
into which I looked and saw
the sky full of stars and the waves
of mountain ranges far below.

A Forlorn Dog

While jobless,
I used to climb the mountain
of our town's Shinto shrine nearby
and look down on a crowd of people
hurrying to their jobs.

Then as I lay on the grass,
looking up at a
Siberian kite, as always
a forlorn dog approached me
and breathed upon my face.

A Fox

Early this morning I found the footprints
Of a fox on the snow in front of my house.
It apparently had passed there just a short time ago.
I decided to trace them.

They went into the woods,
Climbed up the hill and down
Into the valley, under whose snow cover
A thread of water needles through.

The footprints went across it, then
Climbed up again and entered the woods
Deeper. I gave up following them and
Kept on standing, listening to

A faint sound of water beneath my feet.
Then I felt something behind the trees beyond
Looking toward me. But after a while I turned my back
On it and left. It, too, turned its back, quietly leaving.

Section IV:

Breath of God

*"I do not attempt . . .
to provide a proof for Christian faith,
but I will be very happy if I have helped readers to feel,
however faintly,
the breath of God."*

A Hand

Reaching from the other world
Pours tea into my cup.

Inside Me—Before I Was Born

A great tree is growing
its roots deep in the earth
it stretches itself
its heart pounds

It sends out its twigs and branches
like blood vessels into the sky—
the big branches sigh comfortably
wrapped in their luxuriant foliage

At times someone shakes the tree with violent force
then the winds gather,
pile up, envelop it

The clouds are cut up
and blown away
by the wind
all at once the little birds
take flight
desperately I cling
to the trunk

Even after I die
the tree will continue to grow in me—
even now, the faint tremblings
of its leaves

make me quiver
as in a gentle breeze

(This poem, as well as the following five, were translated by Ross L. Bender as were "Joseph . . . " [page 99] and "Testimony . . . " [page 100]).

Jesus' Birth

When waves of pain contort Mary's body
her face is cramped and pale
Her eyes scuttle apart like crabs
The waves pull, recede again

and attack more violently
She clings to the wagon wheel,
grits her teeth, and her screams
terrify the beasts in the stable

Joseph, pacing nervously,
stumbles and falls
At last, seated, he strokes her back,
grasps her hand; his strength flows into her

Then a tremendous power moves within Mary
Like the sun emerging from a mountain ravine
the infant's head appears slowly, deliberately
Joseph grips it in both hands

Now the baby's cry flies out, rends the night
Joseph's doubts dissolve
On the straw bed
Mary peacefully shuts her eyes.

In the Stable

The shepherds have come running
gasping ferociously
They murmur felicitations

The troubled cows and horses
are suddenly cheered; a horse whinnies
and brandishes its tail like a whip

Joseph's fearful face
brightens like a sunflower
with missing teeth

The strain melts from Mary's face
She stretches out and gently holds
her overflowing breasts

Among all the peering faces
the infant sleeps without a sound
The wind slips in for a peek

Peter's Testimony

I didn't expect
a carpenter's son
to know about fish
But his words had
indisputable strength

When I threw in my net
half-doubting, half-believing,
where he showed me
the fish came teeming in
an immense shoal

That tangible, immediate result
—a net so heavy
I could scarcely pull it in—
makes me tremble even now
when I recall his words

Testimony of the Gerasene Demoniac

When that man's footsteps approached
the demons inside me hushed
then suddenly roared

"Come out!" The sound reverberated inside me
and hurled me to the ground; the demons,
fur bristling, rushed out one by one

The pigs surged down the cliff to the lake
Their screams as they drowned resounded for a time
When I came to myself, he was standing

near me
My body was light
As though soft breezes were blowing through

Lazarus' Testimony

When I was steadily
being swallowed by the dark
behind me a voice thundered
"La-za-rus!"
It came flying and seized me

When I returned to the light
summoned by that voice
there before me stood the speaker
His face was like the sky

He peered at me anxiously
When that warm breath
breathed in my face
I realized he had been calling to me
since before I was born

Told by One of the Crowd

I went to the hill
of Golgotha
with a lunch and a deck of cards
as if to a play

I was looking
at those three hung,
exposed to the sun,
blood dripping

and they were panting,
agonizing, sinking exhausted . . .
When tired of looking
we played chess and gambled.

I didn't know
one of them was
a Son of God
and even today

I wouldn't be able to
recognize him, even if
the same thing may happen
again in front of my eyes.

An Outdoor Play

Judas Iscariot, finally freed from the plot,
came to the spring,
easing his throat
and washing his body.

Behind him
the drama
is approaching its climax
but his role is done.

All he is supposed to do
after this
is to hang himself
offstage.

Joseph of Arimathea's Testimony

I picked off the crown of thorns
that had slid over his nose

I pulled blood-crusted nails
out of his wrists

I lifted his stiffened body
from the cross

I closed his mouth and eyes, smeared
balm on his wounds, wrapped him in cloth

I buried him in a tomb
where no one had been buried

What my hands touched was assuredly
The crucified body of Jesus

Testimony of Two Disciples

On the Emmaus road
without realizing it
we spoke with Jesus—told him
what had happened in the capital
complained about the absence of God

We never recognized
this familiar figure
this familiar voice
When we arrived at the village
we sat down to eat, and then

our eyes opened
We saw the one we were with
was Jesus
So preoccupied with
human thoughts

we never dreamt
the man who died
was walking with us
how often will he walk with us
on the road?

Perhaps not until the great banquet at world's end
will we know how many times he has walked with us

Feast of Heaven

I had a duty in Jerusalem at that time
And was on my way there. I certainly
Witnessed a man attacked by robbers
Lying on the roadside severely wounded.

But I was in a hurry and
Didn't want to be bothered by him.
So I walked on by on the other side
As if I had not noticed him.

I don't remember if I felt sorry for him;
This kind of thing happened to me often.
I don't remember if my conscience bothered me;
It happened so many years ago.

But now at this time of ending I peer
Into the feast and am dumbfounded to find
The host in the center is that very man
Who was miserably lying on the roadside.

Jeremiah

He wants to keep his mouth shut,
But somehow placed
Upon his tongue are words,
Which quickly start to burn.
He tries hard to spit them out in a hurry,
But the tongue cramps
And the voices fly out as arrows of fire,
Attacking the people nearby,
Scooping out what they want to hide.

The people first frown, but soon
Their faces twitch.
They shut their ears and try to shake it off.
But the voices enter through
Every pore of their bodies.
They finally explode,   .
Grab Jeremiah, knock him down, and hold his mouth.

—Today as usual, fleeing from their pursuit,
he hides himself in the darkness,
groaning.
"Cursed be the day of my birth!"
"Mother, why did you bear me?"
"God, why do I have to do all these things?
Leave me alone please!
I even do not know how to speak!"

But even while he is thus appealing,
The words are put in his mouth without his knowing,
Which quickly burn and are ready
To fly out! He tries hard to keep his mouth tightly
Shut but it starts writhing.
Jeremiah will be in danger.
His life will be sought after even by his government.

Section V:

Words Made Flesh

"I write today as if it were my last word.
I write today as if I die tomorrow."

Naming

A child says, "Bird,"
Then one quickly flies
down beside him out of nowhere,

He says, "Animal,"
Then one quickly runs to-
ward him from beyond the horizon.

And he is filled with wonder
As he timidly utters the words
and sees them come.

In the garden on the hill
I used to speak in amazement
like that child when I was a child

Words

Leave them there
in the darkness

as they have been
from the beginning.

It's their silences
that speak to us

and not
the combined sounds.

*Note: "Words," just above, and the following two poems, "Many Winds"
and "Gravestones," were set to music for choir and clarinet by composer
Jacques Desjardins.*

Many Winds

Many winds
swarm to
a wounded word,
picking at it
like vultures

until it becomes
a white bone,
half buried in the
sand, and sharpens
into a razor

Gravestones

I caught some words,
which were raging hard
in my hands to flee away,

> but finally I pinned them
> down on a sheet of paper.

There they were writhing,
groaning in death agony,
under the pins of letters,

> but gradually their wings stopped convulsing
> and they were changed into gravestones.

Finally

The words are
all
gone back . . .

The sky

empty . . .

What remains
is

their chaff . . .

Flying

in the empty air
are the shadows of words . . .

Someone is shooting
At them . . .

At Ojima, Matsushima

standing still
before the words

on the weathered stone
almost in-

decipherable
with moss,

i hear
between the waves

the breeze
in the pines

Prayer

The words
stick in my throat

I can't
spit them out

I try to swallow
They won't go down

(This poem was translated by Ross L. Bender, as were the following two poems, "Someone," and "Formerly.")

Someone

From afar
he threw a word like an ax

It cut to pieces
the night's empty sky

It pierced
my unprepared heart

In an instant the ice split
water danced up like a fish

Formerly

Once, I mimicked a missionary,
expounding on repentance
and sin

My tongue fluttered delicately
words danced
like chaff

But now, one by one
on the tip of my tongue
they're as heavy as the earth

When finally I shake one—
push it out—it falls—
heavily—and covers me

Dreams

in the wood
behind my house
is a tree
on which
the tired words and
the wounded words
rest and dream

some are young
and some are aged

tonight
their dreams come
unbidden
into my dreams

They Go Away

I beckon
to the scattered words, "Gather!"
but they don't come.

They perch on twigs
and on grasses,
never heeding.

I run after,
catch some and try to
arrange them in order.

But they won't stay put,
and quickly move
into disorder and go away.

Finally I give up,
lie down on the grass
and keep looking up at the sky.

On the Beach

Walking on the beach, I find
so many words spoken frivolously
during those boisterous days thrown away
like paper scraps and empty cans.

Blown by the wind, some are
swallowed in the wave and others
buried in the sand, and my job is to
collect them in trash cans and

clean the beach. But once in a
rare while, I find one
so deeply buried that even
my violent kicking fails to move it.

So with my shovel I dig deep and
strain to turn it up, then
I find so many hands
of the dead clinging to it.

It's Over

"Hi, everybody! It's all
O-V-E-R!"
Someone shouted on the mountain.

Then all the animals
took off
their animal shapes

and came out,
saying, "Ah, it's
finally over."

I also took off
what I had been wearing
and went to meet them.

To Live Happily

We trap God,
Hang Him
In stained glass,
Entrance Him
By organ music
And chorus.

We bind Him
By ritual,
Tickle him
By prayers
And train Him
To become our pet.

And we freely
Make Him
Take off
Our guilt
Of exploiting
Too much,

Of having
Too much,
Of wasting
Too much,
Of living
Too comfortably.

Once the desert God,
Jealous
And wild;
Now an amulet
On a charm
Bracelet.

Jesus Did Not Come Down

The soldiers clothed him in a
Faded purple uniform,
Mocked him "Hail, King of the Jews,"
And spat upon him.
He did not turn away, but silently endured.

The soldiers put on him
A crown of thorns,
Mocked him, "Hail, King of the Jews,"
And spat upon him.
He did not turn away, but silently endured.

The soldiers knelt down
In mock homage to him,
Then stood up, laughing out.
Finally they nailed him on the cross.
He did not turn away, but silently endured.

The soldiers, the crucified robbers, and the spectators
Looked at crucified Jesus and
Reviled him, "Come down from the cross
That we may see and believe."
He did not come down.

A Tree

When they saw a tree for the first time,
What kind of wonder
Did they have?

Why did they call it
"tree," rather than "river"?
When this sound first came out,

Did they think it
Exactly expressed their feelings?
Were they filled with joy?

To see if there still remains
Their first wonder,
I pick up their word and listen—

Then from the world beneath sound
Their sighs and the word's faint trembling
Float to the shores of my ears.

Editor's note: the next three poems are Yaguchi collaborations with other poets.

One-Line Renga

(In this sequence, from Poetry Nippon, *summer 1982, Yaguchi joins James Kirkup and Mokuo Nagayama in a rotating sequence of traditional one-line "renga.")*

At night a windbell chiming summer sadness.   *Kirkup*

Outside the mosquito net hangs a misty moon.   *Nagayama*

The cosmos faintly shaking; the dawn breeze.   *Yaguchi*

On the horizon, a slow egg soundless breaks.   *Kirkup*

A teacher gazing at his pointer tip: autumn dusk.   *Nagayama*

A horse in the field neighing; the evening bells.   *Yaguchi*

Wild geese migrating form the character for *ku*.   *Kirkup*

Only the sick can fathom the depth of space.   *Nagayama*

The moon above the ruined fortress; an old Ainu kneeling.
                              Yaguchi
Hunger vigil for Kim Dae Jung: Taro Okamoto's foolish clock.
                              Kirkup

Time frozen up, a man waits for his date in vain.   *Nagayama*

Behind the fascinating snow statues, the weapons are hidden.
                              Yaguchi
The mountain peak is red-hot iron.   *Kirkup*

In the dark, a snake in a rage swells and stands.   *Nagayama*

Urinating on the field, a ladybug lands on my penis.   *Yaguchi*

And a neutron bomb irradiates my every vein.   *Kirkup*

Editor's note: This poem appeared in Christian Science Monitor, *December 4, 1984, with the following note: "A Japanese form: odd numbered lines by Yorifumi Yaguchi, even numbered by William Stafford."*

By the Memorial Gate

Sitting, I am waiting for the trees to speak
their silver word, but the moon is late.
The insects are in the grass breathing
for us, for the world, for the stars.
Then, from the heart of the forest, the rippling of leaves
    is approaching
and the whole bright gift of life has come.

Editor's note: This poem, written in collaboration with Robert Bly, appeared in the August 1998 issue of Poetry *magazine.*

Listening to a Storyteller
— In Memoriam William Stafford —

Yaguchi:
In an Ainu house an old Ainu
Woman's recital was flying like bees.

Bly:
Her voice brought honey into the room,
And the bees were preserved in that honey.

Yaguchi:
Honey tastes of wildflowers, out of which
The songs of the bush-warblers come flying.

Bly:
There is water dripping in the deep forests;
And the gods eat the cries of the bush-warblers.

Yaguchi:
There is a deep well covered by grasses;
And I remember the womb I was in.

Bly:
No one knows the silence of the high peaks.
But I sometimes hear Stafford's voice in the bushes.

Yaguchi:
Suddenly silence flies up in the form
Of a bird from a bush nearby.

Bly:
I think the dead spend a lot of time
During the day in the nests of shy birds.

Section VI:

War and Peace

"Poetry is like an arrow.
An arrow coated with poison and medicine."

The Image

in the eyes
of a young airman
shooting down
is
no
longer
of enemies
but of deer
running
away
into a bush

At

a sign
an old couple tri-
ed
to s-
mile at
the camera,

their toothless mouths
cra-
cked and the
bats flew
out

The Party

"Seems some child is crying
In a foreign place," they say with
Smiles over champagne, and their party
Grows cheerful with the music of their band
Raising its volume to
Try to kill that cry.

Then, well-shaped gentlemen begin to
Dance with ladies with half-naked
Mounted breasts. Chandeliers shine
Like many suns, with the marble floor
Flashing like a mirror.

"Oh, how beautiful! Oh
How . . . "

They do not hear any more,
They who dance, laugh and are intoxicated
Hear no more the cry of a child in a land
Beyond the sea. They hear no more
The explosions of
Guns, grenades and bombs they made.

They are dancing, elegantly
Smiling, gradually embracing each other
More tightly, and continue to
Dance through the night.

How to Eat Loaches*
—Some people say raw loaches are good for the heart

You just swallow
the loaches living
without chewing them.

They fall right
into your stomach where
they moan, struggle and

try to jump out.
But they gradually become
faint and still

like mice in a
snake or a minority race
in a society

*a loach is a small fish in the carp family,
sometimes swallowed for medicinal purposes*

At Westminster Abbey

After the overwhelming storm of admiration
At this gorgeous, beautiful and solemn building,
Gradually a wall of cold silence comes around me,
And to my eyes now accustomed to the darkness

Begin to appear those vacant chairs for soldiers
Killed for Great Britain during the wars. And
At the same time come to my ears through the wall-silences
The voiceless cries of agonies, the number of them,

Oh I can tell, I don't know how,
But they are not from the dead sleeping under the ground
Of this Abbey, but from afar, yes coming from
Far over seven seas—

England, oh England. I can't help remembering
What you have done in Africa and in Asia through the centuries,
Though I don't want to do it in this sacred place of yours,
I can't help imagining those enslaved coloreds carrying

Burdens with their slender legs stepping heavily
Deep into burning sand, whipped mercilessly and moaning.
And you have done it in the name of Christ,
The Lord of love and peace.

Do not misunderstand me, I do love you, England,
Your refined culture, but I can never drive away
This very thought that it was surely built by blood-stained
    hands,
By extorted money, by the sacrifices of others.

I, standing alone in the darkness of this Abbey and looking at
Marvelous marbles, shining chandeliers and the queen's
Coronation stand, now can but wonder
How much blood was shed and how much robbed to buy them.

You may say it is the bias of a tiny, prejudiced
Oriental visitor, coming from his inferiority complex.
Maybe so. But come here a little and listen
With me a little. Can't you hear? Or are your ears

Too dull? Calloused? But I can hear, oh now
How vividly I can hear those silent cries—death agonies
Become a grudge swelling in and around the Abbey,
Pouring out of all the bounds of time and space.

I can move no more, but, standing still upon this
Blood-soaked marble, only watch, perplexed, my fellow-visitor,
An aged Japanese, professor of English literature, standing
Still in front of the poets' corner, eyes with tears overfilled.

Prague on August 20, 1968

ah what is it that changed you
so much in one night?
yesterday you were so kind to us
but today you are like a wet stone

when we smiled at you
you smiled back at us o our friends
when we spoke to you
you spoke back to us o our comrades

but now no more
you never smile on us
you never salute us
except with your muzzles

ah what is it that changed your
gentle eyes into such callous eyes,
your soft, warm hands into such
bony fingers on the triggers?

Pendulum

The terror of
Abel,
the first betrayed
and killed

The terror of
Cain,
the first to betray
and kill

Between two terrors
we swing
like a pendulum

(This poem, as well as the following four—"Soldier," "Onlooker," "Follow," and "Public"—were translated by Ross L. Bender.)

Third Soldier's Account

Even if that man was the Christ
it wasn't my fault

I only followed
my officer's orders

Besides, the death sentence was pronounced
by god-fearing people after a fair trial

First Onlooker's Account

With picnic hampers and playing cards
we set out
for the hill of Golgotha
as though to see an outdoor play

Three men
bleached in the sun
blood dripped
they panted and groaned

We noticed they looked
dead tired
as we played chess
or gambled to pass the time

Someone said one of them
was really the Son of God
But I wasn't sure
And even now

I'm not certain
Even if
I'd see the same scene
before my eyes—

To Follow Christ

To become a Christian
is to renounce ancestor worship
or *Jizosama**

There are Christians who in their later years
return to ancestral religion
I think of Suzukisan who was a Christian

but late in life painted only Buddhist pictures
or Satosan who was buried in Buddhist fashion
and is offered incense every morning

I too in recent days have been momentarily charmed
by the Buddha's serene face
rather than the suffering Christ's

But it was gods and buddhas who
once stirred up
militarist passions in me

It is the Christ, the Prince of Peace
whom I continue to follow
who was killed, but did not kill

* *Popular roadside deity, guardian of children*

In the Public Bath

A cross around his neck
a tattooed flower on his back
he plopped into the bath
without washing his lower half

Rubbing his face with a towel
scrubbing the nape of his neck
he shut his eyes as if in a trance
and hummed a tune

On his chest
swaying delicately
on the decorative cross
Jesus hung crucified again

A Nightmare

Those dead
in soldiers' uniforms
became alive

without our knowing
and began to give
orders aloud.

"Isn't this
a nightmare?"
I muttered to myself

but people around me
started
obeying their orders.

"They are supposed to be dead!"
I shouted in confusion
but it was too late.

All of them
picked up their guns
with their eyes glittering.

Suddenly

the wind ripped
the grass and exposed

a snake raising
its head over the nest—

just a vision of the moment—
and the grass was in a hurry

to sew the rip up
in the world of old peace

The Just War

You, who once were missionaries to us,
now attack us,
because your country is
at war with ours.

You bomb our cities,
towns and villages
where you once spread
the good news and built our churches.

"Let every person be subject
to the governing authorities,"
you once taught us.
So, we too attack you,

because our government bids us to.
We bombard you for our country
as you bombard us for your country,
both in the name of our God. Hallelujah!

At the Military Museum

At the military museum were assembled
artifacts of the Imperial Japanese Army.
While standing in front of a bullet display,
an old man came up to me.

"Yup, this round bullet is R-R-Russian-made;
it shatters the bone
'N th-th-this slender one is Japanese,"
the old man began explaining.
"The ones we used were the slender ones;
they really flew—they really hit."
The old guy was hard of hearing, his tongue
twisting, words erupting in little geysers.

"I was dr-dr-drafted. Got to be corporal."
"Did you kill anyone?"
"Yeah, when you'd shoot, the e-e-enemy would
fall over 'n you'd know . . . "

"Yup and this here is a saber—only officers
could have 'em; they'd kill prisoners of war
with them every day'n if they weren't good,
it was bad: they'd hack away'n the neck would dangle."

"Yeah, we'd use our guns every day. If you hit 'em
right, a shot would go right through 'em 'n they
were gone like that. We'd run 'em through with bayonets,
too. You'd b-b-blindfold those guys . . . "

"We had the live prisoners bury the dead ones, a
real big help. I musta killed a hunderd. Ha ha ha . . . "
Usually veterans of the Imperial Army, except for stories
about their own wounds, kept their mouths shut about the war.

This old man had long hidden
all this deep inside;
Senility was beginning to loosen
the strings on the past.

The museum visitors stood around listening;
a Self Defense Force guard on duty also silently attended.
The old man boastfully laughed on, his face twisting; from
the depths of his dark mouth words came popping out
    like frogs.

(translated by Mary Cender Miller)

Martha*

My father was a soldier. He was a sergeant when he quit the Army. He is now a high school teacher in Florida. It's my father who wanted me to have the experience of a soldier. When I was a child, he often encouraged me to join the Navy in my youth. He said that I could travel the whole world free and besides could find a nice husband.

Sir, is it safe here? Someone is chasing me . . . . I am scared . . . . Is someone knocking on the door?

So when I finished high school, I applied for the Navy and became a Marine. Soon I was sent to a small island in the Pacific. For the first couple of weeks, everything was new and exciting. It was fun. During the Pacific War, the Japanese warships were destroyed almost completely near this island, I hear. It took me only 2 hours to walk from one side to the other side. There were about 2000 Marines there. There were no native people. There was only the base there.

Sir, is it safe here? Someone is chasing me . . . . I am scared . . . . Is someone knocking on the door?

What did I do there? There was nothing to do. I got up at five-thirty in the morning. Breakfast was at six-thirty. Then I worked. I cleaned the floor and toilet. I cleaned the boat, too. Cleaning all day! And everyday! Training? Boys were shooting sometimes. We females were cleaning almost all the time, though only occasionally we ran, crawled, and shot pistols. I did not like to use a pistol.

Sir, is it safe here? Someone is chasing me . . . . I am scared . . . . Is someone knocking on the door?

Boring! This describes the very life of this island. There was a ratio of fifteen boys to one girl. Our pleasures were sex, alcohol, drugs, and rock'n'roll. One girl could sleep with as many boys as she wanted. She could sleep with different boys every night. Of course, girls sometimes became pregnant. Girls thought it an honor to be pregnant and to have a baby. It was often difficult to tell who was the father. So, they became unmarried mothers. If the girl was fortunate, she could marry. But normally they soon divorced. Me? I was never pregnant, although I slept with many boys. About forty or fifty. You know, I was in the Navy base for four years. If I did not have sex with them, I would have died of boredom in this place.

Sir, is it safe here? Someone is chasing me . . . . I am scared . . . . Is someone knocking on the door?

I became an alcoholic there. Once I started drinking, I could not stop. If I didn't drink, my whole body began trembling and wouldn't stop. Everybody there was like me. Either an alcoholic or a drug addict . . . . Most of the Marines were farm boys. They had been jobless. So they applied for the Navy. Some of them were attracted by the slogan, "Let us become Marines and see the world free!" Country boys are good-natured, but they are rough like pigs. They make awful sounds, snivel, and splash soup when they eat. City boys are bad boys. They are ill-natured. They always shout angrily and curse others.

Sir, is it safe here? Someone is chasing me . . . . I am scared . . . . Is someone knocking on the door?

We never read books. We were changed into unthinking animals. There were some who wanted to learn skills. They hoped to find jobs after they quit the Navy. But they seldom learned skills because what they were supposed to do was train to become killers. They could quit the Navy, but they would return there again. They could not get along well outside the base.

They are made into such people. Since boys could not satisfy their sexual desires there, they wanted to visit other countries on U.S. ships. When they went to the Philippines, for example, they quickly found girls and slept with them. They wanted to marry them. Any women were O.K. with them.

Sir, is it safe here? Someone is chasing me . . . . I am scared . . . .
Is someone knocking on the door?

It was all boring there. So when there is news that a war may break out somewhere, they are excited and shout with joy. You know, there was a time when the U.S. almost started to attack Iran. At that time they drank, sang, and danced all night, shouting, "Let's go there right now and fight!" I could not do that. I could not continue to be there. I quit the Navy and came to Japan. I was hoping to find a good job here. But I could not . . . . Chaplain? Oh, yes, there was a chaplain there. His face was always red. He smelled of alcohol always. I went to him for counseling, but he said that his worry was much bigger than mine and that he wanted me to hear it. My church is a Southern Baptist church. All the pastors I went to for counseling in the States told me that the Navy was a wonderful place and blessed me.

Sir, is it safe here? Someone is chasing me . . . . I am scared . . . .
Is someone knocking on the door?

* "Martha"and "A Military Nurse"represent recent explorations by Yaguchi based on his visits to hospitals housing aging World War II military nurses and assistants—expressions in prose poems.

140

A Military Nurse

In room 17 of a hospital in the North Ward of Sapporo
An old woman patient begins to shout,
"Look! A head lying down here!"
Her eyes are wide open, her fingers trembling.

"A head there! A head beside my feet, too!
Heads lying all over! All
Staring at me! Help! I'm scared!" Though she can't
Stand alone, she struggles hard to flee.

She is Shioyama Kiyono, 84 years old, who was a
Military nurse for the Japanese army invading China.
She was right in the middle of the Nanjing Massacre.
After the war, she repatriated to Sapporo, but she never

Mentioned what she had seen in China, not even to her family,
Probably because she had been ordered not to.
But now attacked by senility, those memories,
Hidden forcibly beneath her consciousness, have begun to
    fly out.

"Are you going to shoot his brains out, Sir!?"
"Blood scattered all over my white uniform!"
"Are you going to cut his head off, Sir!?" "Look! The intestines
Are oozing out!" "A sea of blood is all over!" "Please! Please

Stop it!" Her face twists and her eyes,
Gazing at emptiness, are bloodshot.
The dark cries fly out from her throat
In big convulsions and small, attacking her alternately.

Held by her family and nurse, she is consoled.
With her back gently rubbed, she gains a little calmness.
Given a shot, she goes off into an ephemeral peace.
But even in this sleep

The figures of those murdered, and the figures of those
Japanese soldiers murdering, appear again.
Is there anyone who can free her from these memories?
Anyone who can give her peace?

I can hear the laughter of those scholars and politicians
Who claim over wine that there was no such thing as a
    massacre,
But here is a woman who continues to suffer the
Nightmares even now when the new millennium has started.

Hanna's Story*

Of course we prayed.
We had been taught that
God would surely come to help us
If we earnestly pray.

Torah says that God will
Protect us. So, everyday,
Day and night we prayed together
And asked Him to save us.

But He did not come at all.
We vainly watched the smoke going up
From the chimneys. Meanwhile
Mother fell ill and was carried away.

Her enfeebled deep eyes
Watched us from the stretcher.
Soon after, Sister became unable to
Stand and was carried away.

My hair began to fall out and
Dizziness attacked me.
Finally I was freed by the advancing
Russian army which destroyed the Germans.

Doesn't God exist? If He does,
He should have come to rescue us.
If God exists, why didn't He come?
Does God even exist now?

I do not understand.
I repeat this question over and over.
But God remains silent.
He never answers me.

Based on a visit Yaguchi made to Israel, this poem expresses his interest in the impact of war and injustice on people, especially women and children, throughout the world.

God of War

God of war, sometimes visible and invisible,
Showed up after his work of Terrorism,
Stood on the platform with his baton,

And started conducting.
Then the U.S. high-tech vultures rushed to Afghan
And started unsparing bombardment.

His seeds bore splendid fruit again!
Joy danced on his face.
This god, who has been worshiped

In the mosques
Under the mask of Allah
And in the church

Under the mask of Christ,
Has been ceaselessly whispering to them
"Make wars."

Now so showily waved he his baton
Both camps responded in ecstatic unison,
"Kill them! Kill them!"

As he conducted more, their hatred
Increased more. His kingdom had been
The battlefield, but now it is the whole globe.

Even when he stopped conducting and disappeared,
He never failed to sow his seeds again.
It is this God who entices us,

"Go to war! Kill them!
I will install you
In my Yasukuni shrine as gods,

As I did before." And our prime minister
Half-rising, is almost ready
To follow him, like a patient infected with high fever.

In My Garden

Refugees come to my garden
where the grasses without insecticide
grow unweeded; a legless katydid,
an armless cricket, a wingless grasshopper,
a snail with its broken shell . . .

After a few nights
they are able to start
a kind of tuning up. Tonight
when the harvest moon floats
high at the center of the sky,

I leave my windows all open
and am attracted through the night
by the maimed orchestra
while my house keeps floating
on the waves of the surrounding grasses.

Something Like a Wind

What I have been trying to catch
In the net of words
Is something like a wind
Coming from another world and
Freely flying
Almost unreachable.

About the Editor

Wilbur Birky was professor of English at Goshen (IN) College from 1964-2002. It was in that role that he first learned to know Yorifumi Yaguchi. The two have been friends and professional colleagues since 1976.

At the invitation of Yaguchi, Birky was Visiting Professor of English at Hokusei Gakuen University in Sapporo, Japan in 1977-78.

In 1986, Birky was Visiting Professor of English and American Literature at the Foreign Language University in Chongqing, China. He has also lectured at Sichuan Teachers' University in China.

Birky's Ph.D. in English is from the University of Iowa. He concluded his formal career in education as Director of International Education at Goshen College.